A Garland Series

The Feminist Controversy in England 1788-1810

A collection of 44 interesting
and important works reprinted
in photo-facsimile in 89 volumes

edited by
Gina Luria
Rutgers University

Thoughts on the Education of Daughters

with Reflections on Female Conduct, in the More Important Duties of Life

Mary Wollstonecraft

with an introduction
for the Garland edition by
Gina Luria

Garland Publishing, Inc., New York & London

1974

Bibliographical note:

This facsimile has been made from a copy in the
Beinecke Library of Yale University
(Lfk14.787W)

Library of Congress Cataloging in Publication Data

Wollstonecraft, Mary, 1759-1797.
   Thoughts on the education of daughters.

   (The Feminist controversy in England, 1788-1810)
   Reprint of the 1787 ed. printed for J. Johnson,
London.
   Bibliography: p.
   1. Women--Social and moral questions. 2. Young
women. I. Title. II. Series.
HQ1229.W85 1974   301.41'2   74-8251
ISBN 0-8240-0890-1

Printed in the United States of America

Introduction

Mary Wollstonecraft (1759-1797) was born in Yorkshire. The unhappiness of her family life soon drove her to seek independence. Though she attended day school in Yorkshire, her husband William Godwin noted in his *Memoir* of her that "it was not to any advantage of infant literature, that she was indebted for her subsequent eminence." Her real education in the teachings of the Enlightenment *philosophes* probably began during her informal tutelage with Dr. Richard Price, a leading radical Dissenter and a member of the Dissenting colony at Newington Green where Wollstonecraft and her sisters established a school in 1783. In her biographical sketch of Wollstonecraft in *Shelley and his Circle* (Volume I, 1961), Eleanor Nicholes suggests that one of the pivots of Wollstonecraft's later thought — her belief that "truth was to be discovered, or validated, by searching into one's own experiences and thoughts upon the meaning of those experiences" — derived from her connection with Price and the Rational Dissenters.

Certainly, Mary Wollstonecraft's erudition remains an enigma as much today as when her dazzling *Vindication of the Rights of Woman* was first published in 1792. Her contemporary, student, and close friend, the novelist Mary Hays, expressed the mystery of the genesis of Wollstonecraft's genius in an obituary written several years after her death.

> That something could be added respecting the earlier progress of a mind thus gifted, is to be wished rather than expected; the growth of intellect and the rise of ideas are rarely to be traced. On this subject we have no authority; but are inclined to suspect, that, like the majority of her sex, her studies were desultory and her attainments casual, pursued with little method, under the direction of her taste, or as her feelings took the lead.

Mary Wollstonecraft's personal and creative history continues to be the focus of critical attention. The works reprinted in the present series

6

include three of her least recognized efforts. The first of these, *Thoughts on the Education of Daughters* (1787), is generally regarded as an immature, awkward, and stoic literary attempt. In his biography of Wollstonecraft (1951), Ralph Wardle describes the book as "obviously a pot-boiler scribbled off for the sake of the ten guineas which it would yield," but points to its interest for the student of Wollstonecraft's work in that "in some respects *Thoughts* foreshadowed Mary's later work in *The Rights of Woman.* . . . Her book shows that she was dissatisfied with the status of her sex, but that as yet she had not formulated her objections or traced them to the basic human rights to which women as well as men were entitled." The work is interesting as well for its reflection of Wollstonecraft's responses to contemporary strictures for young women.

Another early work, *Mary; A Fiction* (1788), is reprinted for its interest as Wollstonecraft's youthful attempt at novel writing and for its innovative content. As Wollstonecraft herself writes in the "Preface" to the book, "In delineating the Heroine of this Fiction, the Author attempts to develop a

character different from those generally por-
trayed." Most striking is her specific aim: "in an
artless tale, without episodes, the mind of a woman
who has thinking powers is displayed." As Eleanor
Nicholes suggests, there are several elements in
Mary which anticipated "much of the attitude and
tone of the Romantic period," during which
Shelley and his second wife, Mary Wollstonecraft's
daughter, Mary Wollstonecraft Godwin, flourished.
These elements include the "intensely personal"
style, the striking connection between nature and
conscious man (significantly represented here by
conscious *woman*), and the "portrait" of the
"content of consciousness" of the heroine's mind.

Although available in modern editions, a facsimile of the first edition of *The Rights of Woman*
is included in this series because of its central
and seminal place in the feminist controversy of
the 1790s. Women long before Wollstonecraft had
enunciated much of the content — and the spirit —
of her manifesto, but none had galvanized the
attention and the energies of a generation of
middle-class men and women as she did. No doubt
part of the reason for her success was the prevailing

INTRODUCTION

"spirit of the age": the rights of woman, as Wollstonecraft elucidated them, are simply a logical extension of the eighteenth century's understanding of the Rights of Man. For the first time, the fundamental conceptions of democracy were extended to women by a woman; *A Vindication of the Rights of Woman* is a companion-piece to the *Declaration of Independence*. During a brief period, at least, Wollstonecraft's work – and her life – served as a bill of rights for some of her countrywomen and, for a long time afterwards, as a target for attack for many others.

Finally, Wollstonecraft's *Posthumous Works* (1798) are also reprinted for the light they shed on the directions of her maturer thought. Most interesting among the miscellaneous fragments collected are the "Hints" for a companion volume to *The Rights of Woman*, and an unfinished novel, *The Wrongs of Woman, or Maria*. The central metaphor of the work is, in Wollstonecraft's words, "the world [as] a vast prison, and women born slaves." Margaret George in *One Woman's 'Situation'* (1970) describes the book as "a fictional version of *The Rights of Woman*, a sweeping artistically designed account of women in the modern world." Eleanor Flexner in her biography of Wollstonecraft (1972) singles out as one of the strengths of the tale the character of Jemima, the heroine's servant in the insane asylum in which she has been legally incarcerated by her husband. Jemima, writes Flexner, "is something new in English fiction, the kind of character who did not really come to life till the advent of Dickens, a woman who has been hunted from hole to hole. . . . [Wollstonecraft] heralded the existence of the Jemimas and demanded that society recognize their plight and its responsibility for them."

It is the hope of the editor that, by making these lesser works of Wollstonecraft's available, a new aspect of her creative endeavors will come under closer scrutiny, a more imaginative, less doctrinal side that has been treated perhaps too casually.

Gina Luria

Select Bibliography

There are numerous studies of Mary Wollstonecraft in addition to the ones mentioned. Charles Hagelman, Jr., provides a partial bibliography in his edition of Wollstonecraft's *Rights of Woman* (1967).

Cameron, Kenneth Neill, ed. *Shelley and His Circle, 1773-1822*. Vols. 1 and 2. Cambridge, Mass.: Harvard University Press, 1961.

Flexner, Eleanor. *Mary Wollstonecraft*. New York: Coward, McCann & Geoghegan, 1972.

Luria, Gina. "Mary Hays: A Critical Biography." Unpub. Ph.D. dissertation, New York University, 1971.

Nixon, Edna. *Mary Wollstonecraft: Her Life and Times*. London: J. M. Dent & Sons Ltd., 1971.

Wardle, Ralph. *Mary Wollstonecraft: A Critical Biography*. A Bison Book, 1966.

THOUGHTS

ON THE

EDUCATION

OF

DAUGHTERS:

WITH

REFLECTIONS ON FEMALE CONDUCT,

IN

The more important DUTIES of LIFE.

By MARY WOLLSTONECRAFT.

LONDON:

PRINTED FOR J. JOHNSON, Nº 72, ST. PAUL'S
CHURCH-YARD.

M DCC LXXXVII.

PREFACE.

IN the following pages I have endeavoured to point out some important things with respect to female education. It is true, many treatises have been already written; yet it occurred to me, that much still remained to be said. I shall not swell these sheets by writing apologies for my attempt. I am afraid, indeed, the reflections will, by some, be thought too grave; but I could not make them less so without writing affectedly;

affectedly;

fectedly; yet, though they may be infipid to the gay, others may not think them fo; and if they fhould prove ufeful to one fellow-creature, and beguile any hours, which forrow has made heavy, I fhall think I have not been employed in vain.

THOUGHTS

THOUGHTS

ON THE

EDUCATION

OF

DAUGHTERS.

The NURSERY.

AS I conceive it to be the duty of every rational creature to attend to its offspring, I am sorry to observe, that reason and duty together have not so powerful an influence over

B human

human conduct, as inftinct has in the brute creation. Indolence, and a thoughtlefs difregard of every thing, except the prefent indulgence, make many mothers, who may have momentary ftarts of tendernefs, neglect their children. They follow a pleafing impulfe, and never reflect that reafon fhould cultivate and govern thofe inftincts which are implanted in us to render the path of duty pleafant—for if they are not governed they will run wild; and ftrengthen the paffions which are ever endeavouring to obtain dominion——I mean vanity and felf-love.

The

The first thing to be attended to, is laying the foundation of a good constitution. The mother (if there are not very weighty reasons to prevent her) ought to suckle her children. Her milk is their proper nutriment, and for some time is quite sufficient. Were a regular mode of suckling adopted, it would be far from being a laborious task. Children, who are left to the care of ignorant nurses, have their stomachs overloaded with improper food, which turns acid, and renders them very uncomfortable. We should be particularly careful to guard them in their infant state from bodily pain; as their minds can then afford them no

amufement to alleviate it. The firft
years of a child's life are frequently
made miferable through negligence or
ignorance. Their complaints are moftly in their ftomach or bowels; and
thefe complaints generally arife from
the quality and quantity of their food.

The fuckling of a child alfo excites
the warmeft glow of tendernefs—Its
dependant, helplefs ftate produces an
affection, which may properly be termed maternal. I have even felt it, when
I have feen a mother perform that
office; and am of opinion, that maternal tendernefs arifes quite as much
from habit as inftinct. It is poffible, I

m

am convinced, to acquire the affection of a parent for an adopted child; it is neceſſary, therefore, for a mother to perform the office of one, in order to produce in herſelf a rational affection for her offspring.

Children very early contract the manners of thoſe about them. It is eaſy to diſtinguiſh the child of a well-bred perſon, if it is not left entirely to the nurſe's care. Theſe women are of courſe ignorant, and to keep a child quiet for the moment, they humour all its little caprices. Very ſoon does it begin to be perverſe, and eager to be gratified in every thing. The uſual

B 3 mode

mode of acting is complying with the
humours sometimes, and contradicting
them at others—just according to the
dictates of an uncorrected temper.
This the infant finds out earlier than
can be imagined, and it gives rise to
an affection devoid of respect. Uni-
formity of conduct is the only feasible
method of creating both.   An inflexi-
ble adherence to any rule that has
been laid down makes children comfortable, and saves the mother and
nurse much trouble, as they will not
often contest, if they have not once
conquered.   They will, I am sure,
love and respect a person who treats
them properly, if some one else does

not

not indifcreetly indulge them. I once
heard a judicious father fay, " He
would treat his child as he would his
horfe : firft convince it he was its
mafter, and then its friend." But
yet a rigid ftyle of behaviour is by no
means to be adopted; on the contrary,
I wifh to remark, that it is only in the
years of childhood that the happinefs
of a human being depends entirely on
others—and to embitter thofe years
by needlefs reftraint is cruel. To
conciliate affection, affection muft be
fhown, and little proofs of it ought
always to be given—let them not appear weaknefſes, and they will fink
deep into the young mind, and call

B 4 forth

forth its most amiable propensities.
The turbulent passions may be kept
down till reason begins to dawn.

In the nursery too, they are taught
to speak; and there they not only hear
nonsense, but that nonsense retailed
out in such silly, affected tones as must
disgust;—yet these are the tones which
the child first imitates, and its innocent playful manner renders them
tolerable, if not pleasing; but afterwards they are not easily got the better
of—nay, many women always retain
the pretty prattle of the nursery, and
do not forget to lisp, when they have
learnt to languish.

Children

Children are taught revenge and lies in their very cradles. If they fall down, or ſtrike their heads againſt any thing, to quiet them they are bid return the injury, and their little hands held out to do it. When they cry, or are troubleſome, the cat or dog is chaſtiſed, or ſome bugbear called to take them away; which only terriſies them at firſt, for they ſoon find out that the nurſe means nothing by theſe dreadful threatenings. Indeed, ſo well do they diſcover the fallacy, that I have ſeen little creatures, who could ſcarcely ſpeak, play over the ſame tricks with their doll or the cat.

How,

How, then, when the mind comes under difcipline, can precepts of truth be inforced, when the firft examples they have had would lead them to practife the contrary?

MORAL

MORAL DISCIPLINE.

IT has been afferted, " That no being, merely human, could properly
educate a child." I entirely coincide
with this author; but though perfection cannot be attained, and unfore-
feen events will ever govern human
conduct, yet ftill it is our duty to lay
down fome rule to regulate our actions by, and to adhere to it, as confift-
ently as our infirmities will permit.
To be able to follow Mr. Locke's fyf-
tem (and this may be faid of almoft
all treatifes on education) the parents
muft have fubdued their own paffions,
which

which is not often the cafe in any confiderable degree.

The marriage ftate is too often a
ftate of difcord; it does not always
happen that both parents are rational,
and the weakeft have it in their power
to do moft mifchief.

How then are the tender minds
of children to be cultivated?—
Mamma is only anxious that they
fhould love her beft, and perhaps
takes pains to fow thofe feeds,
which have produced fuch luxuriant
weeds in her own mind. Or, what ftill
more frequently occurs, the children
are at firft made play-things of, and
when

when their tempers have been spoiled by indiscreet indulgence, they become troublesome, and are mostly left with servants; the first notions they imbibe, therefore, are mean and vulgar. They are taught cunning, the wisdom of that class of people, and a love of truth, the foundation of virtue, is soon obliterated from their minds. It is, in my opinion, a well-proved fact, that principles of truth are innate. Without reasoning we assent to many truths; we feel their force, and artful sophistry can only blunt those feelings which nature has implanted in us as instinctive guards to virtue. Dissimulation and cunning will soon drive all other good

good qualities before them, and de-
prive the mind of that beautiful fim-
plicity, which can never be too much
cherifhed.

Indeed it is of the utmoft confequence to make a child artlefs, or to
fpeak with more propriety, not to
teach them to be otherwife; and in
order to do fo we muft keep them out
of the way of bad examples. Art is
almoft always practifed by fervants,
and the fame methods which children
obferve them to ufe, to fhield themfelves from blame, they will adopt—
and cunning is fo nearly allied to falfe-
hood, that it will infallibly lead to it—

I   or

or some foolish prevaricating subter-
fuge will occur, to silence any re-
proaches of the mind which may arise,
if an attention to truth has been inculcated.

Another cause or source of art is in-
judicious correction. Accidents or
giddy tricks are too frequently pu-
nished, and if children can conceal
these, they will, to avoid chastisement.
Restrain them, therefore, but never
correct them without a very sufficient
cause ; such as a violation of truth,
cruelty to animals, inferiors, or those
kind of follies which lead to vice.

Children

Children fhould be permitted to enter into converfation; but it requires
great difcernment to find out fuch
fubje as will gradually improve
them. Animals are the firft objeds
which catch their attention; and I
think little ftories about them would
not only amufe but inftruct at the fame
time, and have the beft effect in forming the temper and cultivating the
good difpofitions of the heart. There
are many little books which have
this tendency. One in particular I
recollect: The Perambulations of a
Moufe. I cannot here help mentioning a book of hymns, in meafured
profe, written by the ingenious author

of

of many other proper leſſons for children. Theſe hymns, I imagine, would
contribute to fill the heart with religious ſentiments and affections; and,
if I may be allowed the expreſſion,
make the Deity obvious to the ſenſes.
The underſtanding, however, ſhould
not be overloaded any more than the
ſtomach. Intellectual improvements,
like the growth and formation of the
body, muſt be gradual—yet there is no
reaſon why the mind ſhould lie fallow,
while its " frail tenement" is imperceptibly fitting itſelf for a more rea-
ſonable inhabitant. It will not lie fallow; promiſcuous ſeeds will be ſown
by accident, and they will ſhoot up

C

with

with the wheat, and perhaps never be eradicated.

Whenever a child afks a queftion, it fhould always have a reafonable anfwer given it. Its little paffions fhould be engaged. They are moftly fond of ftories, and proper ones would improve them even while they. are amufed. Inftead of thefe, their heads are filled with improbable tales, and fuperftitious accounts of invifible beings, which breed ftrange prejudices and vain fears in their minds.

The lifp of the nurfery is confirmed, and vulgar phrafes are acquired; which children, if poffible, fhould never hear.

'To be able to exprefs the thoughts with facility and propriety, is of great con-fequence in life, and if children were never led aftray in this particular, it would prevent much trouble.

The riot too of the kitchen, or any other place where children are left only with fervants, makes the decent reftraint of the parlour irkfome. A girl, who has vivacity, foon grows a romp; and if there are male fervants, they go out a walking with them, and will frequently take little freedoms with Mifs, the bearing with which gives a forwardnefs to her air, and makes her pert. The becoming mo-

defty,

defty, which being accuftomed to converfe with fuperiors, will give a girl,
is entirely done away. I muft own,
I am quite charmed when I fee a fweet
young creature, fhrinking as it were
from obfervation, and liftening rather
than talking. It is poffible a girl may
have this manner without having a very
good underftanding. If it fhould be
fo, this diffidence prevents her from
being troublefome.

It is the duty of a parent to preferve
a child from receiving wrong impref-
fions.—As to prejudices, the firft notions we have deferve that name; for
it is not till we begin to waver in our
opinions,

opinions, that we exert our reafon to
examine them—and then, if they are
received, they may be called our own.

The firft things, then, that children
ought to be encouraged to obferve,
are a ftrict adherence to truth; a
proper fubmiffion to fuperiors; and
condefcenfion to inferiors. Thefe are
the main articles; but there are many
others, which compared to them are
trivial, and yet are of importance. It
is not pleafing to fee a child full of bows
and grimaces; yet they need not be
fuffered to be rude. They fhould be
employed, and fuch fables and tales
may be called out for them as would

     excite

excite their curiofity.   A tafte for the
beauties of nature fhould be very early
cultivated : many things, with refpe&
to the vegetable and animal world,
may be explained in an amufing way ;
and this is an innocent fource of pleafure within every one's reach.

Above all, try to teach them to
combine their ideas.   It is of more ufe
than can be conceived, for a child to
learn to compare things that are fimi-
lar in fome refpe&s, and different in
others.   I wifh them to be taught to
think—thinking, indeed, is a fevere
exercife, and exercife of either mind or
body will not at firft be entered on, but
                                   with

with a view to pleasure. Not that I would have them make long reflections; for when they do not arise from experience, they are mostly absurd.

EX-

[4]

EXTERIOR ACCOMPLISH-
MENTS.

UNDER this head may be ranked all thofe accomplifhments which merely render the perfon attractive; and thofe half-learnt ones which do not improve the mind. " A little learning of any kind is a dangerous thing;" and fo far from making a per-fon pleafing, it has the contrary effect.

Parents have moftly fome weighty weighty bufinefs in hand, which they make a pretext to themfelves for ne-glecting the arduous tafk of educating their children; they are therefore fent

8

to

to fchool, and the allowance for them is fo low, that the perfon who undertakes the charge muft have more than fhe can poffibly attend to; of courfe, the mechanical parts of education can only be obferved. I have known children who could repeat things in the order they learnt them, that were quite at a lofs when put out of the beaten track. If the underftanding is not exercifed, the memory will be employed to little purpofe.

Girls learn fomething of mufic, drawing, and geography; but they do not know enough to engage their attention, and render it an employment of the mind. If they can play over a few

tunes

tunes to their acquaintance, and have
a drawing or two (half done by the
mafter) to hang up in their rooms,
they imagine themfelves artifts for
the reft of their lives. It is not
the being able to execute a trifling
landfcape, or any thing of the kind,
that is of confequence—Thefe are
at beft but trifles, and the foolifh,
indifcriminate praifes which are beftowed on them only produce vanity.
But what is really of no importance,
when confidered in this light, becomes
of the utmoft, when a girl has a fondnefs for the art, and a defire of excel-
lence. Whatever tends to make a
perfon in fome meafure independent

of

of the fenfes, is a prop to virtue. A-
mufing employments muft firft occupy
the mind ; and as an attention to moral duties leads to piety, fo whoever
weighs one fubject will turn to others,
and new ideas will rufh into the mind.
The faculties will be exercifed, and
not fuffered to fleep, which will give a
variety to the character.

Dancing and elegance of manners
are very pleafing, if too great a ftrefs
is not laid on them. Thefe acquire-
ments catch the fenfes, and open the
way to the heart ; but unfupported by
folid good qualities, their reign is fhort.

The lively thoughtleffnefs of youth
makes every young creature agreeable
for

for the time; but when thofe years are flown, and fenfe is not fubftituted in the ftead of vivacity, the follies of youth are acted over, and they never confider, that the things which pleafe in their proper feafon, difguft out of it. It is very abfurd to fee a woman, whofe brow time has marked with wrinkles, aping the manners of a girl in her teens.

I do not think it foreign to the prefent fubject to mention the trifling converfations women are moftly fond of. In general, they are prone to ridicule. As they lay the greateft ftrefs on manners, the moft refpectable characters will

will not escape its lash, if deficient in this article. Ridicule has been, with some people, the boasted test of truth —if so, our sex ought to make wonderful improvements; but I am apt to think, they often exert this talent till they lose all perception of it themselves. Affectation, and not ignorance, is the fair game for ridicule; and even affectation some good-natured persons will spare. We should never give pain without a design to amend.

Exterior accomplishments are not to be despised, if the acquiring of them does not satisfy the possessors, and prevent their cultivating the more important ones.

ARTI-

ARTIFICIAL MANNERS.

IT may be thought, that artificial manners and exterior accomplishments are much the same; but I think the former take a far wider range, and are materially different. The one arises from affectation, and the other seems only an error in judgment.

The emotions of the mind often appear conspicuous in the countenance and manner. These emotions, when they arise from sensibility and virtue, are inexpressibly pleasing. But it is easier to copy the cast of countenance, than to cultivate the virtues which animate and improve it.

How

How many people are like whiten-
ed fepulchres, and careful only about
appearances! yet if we are too anxious to gain the approbation of the
world, we muft often forfeit our own.

How bewitching is that humble foft-
nefs of manners which humility gives
birth to, and how faint are the imi-
tations of affeƈtation! That gentlenefs
of behaviour, which makes us courte-
ous to all, and that benevolence, which
makes us loth to offend any, and
ftudious to pleafe every creature, is
fometimes copied by the polite; but
how aukward is the copy! The
warmeft profeffions of regard are prof-
tituted

tituted on all occasions. No distinctions are made, and the esteem which is only due to merit, appears to be lavished on all—Nay, affection is affected; at least, the language is borrowed, when there is no glow of it in the heart. Civility is due to all, but regard or admiration should never be expressed when it is not felt.

As humility gives the most pleasing cast to the countenance, so from sincerity arises that artlessness of manners which is so engaging. She who suffers herself to be seen as she really is, can never be thought affected. She is not solicitous to act a part; her en-

deavour

deavour is not to hide; but correct her failings, and her face has of courfe that beauty, which an attention to the mind only gives. I never knew a perfon really ugly, who was not foolifh or vicious; and I have feen the moft beautiful features deformed by paffion and vice. It is true, regular features ftrike at firft; but it is a well ordered mind which occafions thofe turns of expreffion in the countenance, which make a lafting impreffion.

Feeling is ridiculous when affected; and even when felt, ought not to be difplayed. It will appear if genuine; but when pufhed forward to notice, it is obvious vanity has rivalled forrow,

D   and

and that the prettineſs of the thing is thought of. Let the manners ariſe from the mind, and let there be no diſguiſe for the genuine emotions of the heart.

Things merely ornamental are ſoon diſregarded, and diſregard can ſcarcely be borne when there is no internal ſupport.

To have in this uncertain world ſome ſtay, which cannot be undermined, is of the utmoſt conſequence; and this ſtay it is, which gives that dignity to the manners, which ſhews that a perſon does not depend on mere human applauſe for comfort and ſatisfaction.

DRESS.

D R E S S.

MANY able pens have dwelt on the peculiar foibles of our sex. We have been equally desired to avoid the two extremes in dress, and the necessity of cleanliness has been insisted on, " As from the body's purity the mind receives a sympathetic aid."

By far too much of a girl's time is taken up in dress. This is an exterior accomplishment; but I chose to consider it by itself. The body hides the mind, and it is, in its turn, obscured by the drapery. I hate to see the frame of a picture so glaring, as to

D 2   catch

catch the eye and divide the attention.
Dreſs ought to adorn the perſon,
and not rival it. It may be ſimple,
elegant, and becoming, without being
expenſive; and ridiculous faſhions diſregarded, while ſingularity is avoided.
The beauty of dreſs (I ſhall raiſe aſto-
niſhment by ſaying ſo) is its not being conſpicuous one way or the other;
when it neither diſtorts, or hides the
human form by unnatural protuber-
ances. If ornaments are much ſtudied,
a conſciouſneſs of being well dreſſed
will appear in the face—and ſurely
this mean pride does not give much
ſublimity to it.

" Out

" Out of the abundance of the heart the mouth ſpeaketh." And how much converſation does dreſs furniſh, which ſurely cannot be very improving or entertaining.

It gives riſe to envy, and conteſts for trifling ſuperiority, which do not render a woman very reſpectable to the other ſex.

Arts are uſed to obtain money; and much is ſquandered away, which if ſaved for charitable purpoſes, might alleviate the diſtreſs of many poor families, and ſoften the heart of the girl who entered into ſuch ſcenes of woe.

D 3 In

In the article of dress may be included the whole tribe of beauty-
washes, cosmetics, Olympian dew, ori-
ental herbs, liquid bloom, and the
paint which enlivened Ninon's face,
and bid defiance to time. These numerous and essential articles are ad-
vertised in so ridiculous a style, that
the rapid sale of them is a very severe
reflection on the understanding of those
females who encourage it. The dew
and herbs, I imagine, are very harm-
less, but I do not know whether the
same may be said of the paint. White
is certainly very prejudicial to the
health, and never can be made to re-
semble nature. The red, too, takes
off

2

off from the expreſſion of the countenance, and the beautiful glow which
modeſty, affection, or any other emotion of the mind, gives, can never be
ſeen. It is not " a mind-illumined
face." " The body does not charm,
becauſe the mind is ſeen," but juſt the
contrary; and if caught by it a man
marries a woman thus diſguiſed, he
may chance not to be ſatisfied with her
real perſon. A made-up face may
ſtrike viſitors, but will certainly diſguſt
domeſtic friends. And one obvious
inference is drawn, truth is not expected to govern the inhabitant of ſo artificial a form. The falſe life with which
rouge animates the eyes, is not of the

D 4 moſt

moſt delicate kind; nor does a woman's dreſſing herſelf in a way to at-
tract languiſhing glances, give us the
moſt advantageous opinion of the purity of her mind.

I forgot to mention powder among
the deceptions. It is a pity that it ſhould
be ſo generally worn. The moſt beautiful ornament of the features is diſguiſed, and the ſhade it would give to the
countenance entirely loſt. The color
of every perſon's hair generally ſuits
the complexion, and is calculated to
ſet it off. What abſurdity then do
they run into, who uſe red, blue, and
yellow powder!—And what a falſe
taſte does it exhibit!

The

The quantity of pomatum is often diſguſting. We laugh at the Hotten-tots, and in ſome things adopt their cuſtoms.

Simplicity of Dreſs, and unaffected manners, ſhould go together. They demand reſpect, and will be admired by people of taſte, even when love is out of the queſtion.

THE

The FINE ARTS.

MUSIC and painting, and many other ingenious arts, are now brought to great perfection, and afford the moft rational and delicate pleafure.

It is eafy to find out if a young perfon has a tafte for them. If they have, do not fuffer it to lie dormant. Heaven kindly beftowed it, and a great bleffing it is; but, like all other bleffings, may be perverted: yet the intrinfic value is not leffened by the perverfion. Should nature have been a niggard to them in this refpect, perfuade

them

them to be filent, and not feign rap-
tures they do not feel; for nothing
can be more ridiculous.

In mufic I prefer expreffion to execution. The fimple melody of fome
artlefs airs has often foothed my mind,
when it has been harraffed by care;
and I have been raifed from the very
depths of forrow, by the fublime harmony of fome of Handel's compofi-
tions. I have been lifted above this
little fcene of grief and care, and mufed
on Him, from whom all bounty flows.

A perfon muft have fenfe, tafte, and
fenfibility, to render their mufic interesting.

resting.   The nimble dance of the
fingers may raise wonder, but not
delight.

As to drawing, those cannot be really
charmed by it, who do not observe the
beauties of nature, and even admire
them.

If a person is fond of tracing the
effects of the passions, and marking the
appearances they give to the countenance, they will be glad to see characters displayed on canvass, and enter
into the spirit of them ; but if by them
the book of nature has not been read,
their admiration is childish.

Works

Works of fancy are very amuſing, if a girl has a lively fancy; but if ſhe makes others do the greateſt part of them, and only wiſhes for the credit of doing them, do not encourage her.

Writing may be termed a fine art; and, I am ſure, it is a very uſeful one. The ſtyle in particular deſerves attention. Young people are very apt to ſubſtitute words for ſentiments, and clothe mean thoughts in pompous diction. Induſtry and time are neceſſary to cure this, and will often do it. Children ſhould be led into correſpondences, and methods adopted to make them write down their ſentiments, and

they

they should be prevailed on to relate
the ſtories they have read in their own
words.   Writing well is of great conſequence in life as to our temporal intereſt, and of ſtill more to the mind;
as it teaches a perſon to arrange their
thoughts, and digeſt them.   Beſides,
it forms the only true baſis of rational
and elegant converſation.

Reading, and ſuch arts as have been
already mentioned, would fill up the
time, and prevent a young perſon's
being loſt in diſſipation, which ener-
vates the mind, and often leads to improper connections.   When habits are
fixed, and a character in ſome meaſure formed, the entering into the
busy

buſy world, ſo far from being dangerous, is uſeful. Knowledge will
imperceptibly be acquired, and the
taſte improved, if admiration is not
more ſought for than improvement.
For thoſe ſeldom make obſervation
who are full of themſelves.

READING.

READING.

IT is an old, but a very true obfervation, that the human mind muſt
ever be employed. A reliſh for reading, or any of the fine arts, ſhould be
cultivated very early in life; and thoſe
who reflect can tell, of what importance it is for the mind to have ſome re-
ſource in itſelf, and not to be entirely
dependant on the ſenſes for employment and amuſement. If it unfortu-
nately is ſo, it muſt ſubmit to mean-
neſs, and often to vice, in order to
gratify them. The wiſeſt and beſt are
too much under their influence; and
the endeavouring to conquer them,

when

when reaſon and virtue will not give
their ſanction, conſtitutes great part of
the warfare of life. What ſupport,
then, have they who are all ſenſes,
and who are full of ſchemes, which
terminate in temporal objects?

Reading is the moſt rational employment, if people ſeek food for the
underſtanding, and do not read merely
to remember words; or with a view
to quote celebrated authors, and re-
tail ſentiments they do not underſtand
or feel. Judicious books enlarge the
mind and improve the heart, though
ſome, by them, " are made coxcombs
" whom nature meant for fools."

F.

Thoſe

Thofe productions which give a wrong account of the human paffions, and the various accidents of life, ought not to be read before the judgment is formed, or at leaft exercifed. Such accounts are one great caufe of the affectation of young women. Senfibility is defcribed and praifed, and the effects of it reprefented in a way fo different from nature, that thofe who imitate it muft make themfelves very ridiculous. A falfe tafte is acquired, and fenfible books appear dull and infipid after thofe fuperficial performances, which obtain their full end if they can keep the mind in a continual ferment. Gallantry is made the only interefting

fubject

subject with the novelist; reading, therefore, will often co-operate to make his fair admirers insignificant.

I do not mean to recommend books of an abstracted or grave cast. There are in our language many, in which instruction and amusement are blended; the Adventurer is of this kind. I mention this book on account of its beautiful allegories and affecting tales, and similar ones may easily be selected. Reason strikes most forcibly when illustrated by the brilliancy of fancy. The sentiments which are scattered may be observed, and when they are relished, and the

mind

mind set to work, it may be allowed to chuse books for itself, for every thing will then instruct.

I would have every one try to form an opinion of an author themselves, though modesty may restrain them from mentioning it. Many are so anxious to have the reputation of taste, that they only praise the authors whose merit is indisputable. I am sick of hearing of the sublimity of Milton, the elegance and harmony of Pope, and the original, untaught genius of Shakespear. These cursory remarks are made by some who know nothing of nature, and could not enter into the

spirit

2

fpirit of thofe authors, or underftand them.

A florid ftyle moftly paffes with the ignorant for fine writing ; many fentences are admired that have no meaning in them, though they contain " words of thundering found," and others that have nothing to recommend them but fweet and mufical terminations.

Books of theology are not calculated for young perfons; religion is beft taught by example. The Bible fhould be read with particular refpect, and they fhould not be taught reading by

E 3   fo

fo facred a book ; left they might confider that as a tafk, which ought to be
a fource of the moft exalted fatisfaction.

It may be obferved, that I recommend the mind's being put into a proper train, and then left to itfelf. Fixed
rules cannot be given, it muft depend
on the nature and ftrength of the underftanding ; and thofe who obferve
it can beft tell what kind of cultiva-
tion will improve it. The mind is not,
cannot be created by the teacher,
though it may be cultivated, and its
real powers found out.

The active fpirits of youth may
make time glide away without intellectual

lectual enjoyments ; but when the novelty of the fcene is worn off, the want
of them will be felt, and nothing elfe
can fill up the void. The mind is
confined to the body, and muft fink
into fenfuality ; for it has nothing to
do but to provide for it, " how it fhall
eat and drink, and wherewithal it fhall
be clothed."

All kinds of refinement have been
found fault with for increafing our
cares and forrows ; yet furely the
contrary effect alfo arifes from them.
Tafte and thought open many fources
of pleafure, which do not depend on
fortune.

E 4 No

No employment of the mind is a sufficient excuse for neglecting domestic duties, and I cannot conceive that they are incompatible. A woman may fit herself to be the companion and friend of a man of sense, and yet know how to take care of his family.

BOARD-

BOARDING-SCHOOLS.

IF a mother has leifure and good fenfe, and more than one daughter, I think fhe could beft educate them herfelf; but as many family reafons render it neceffary fometimes to fend them from home, boarding-fchools are fixed on. I muft own it is my opinion, that the manners are too much attended to in all fchools; and in the nature of things it cannot be otherwife, as the reputation of the houfe depends upon it, and moft people can judge of them. The temper is neglected, the fame leffons are taught to all, and fome get a fmatter-

ing

ing of things they have not capacity
ever to underſtand; few things are
learnt thoroughly, but many follies
contracted, and an immoderate fondnefs for drefs among the reſt.

To prepare a woman to fulfil the
important duties of a wife and mother, are certainly the objects that
ſhould be in view during the early
period of life; yet accompliſhments
are moſt thought of, and they, and all-
powerful beauty, generally gain the
heart; and as the keeping of it is not
confidered of until it is loſt, they are
deemed of the moſt confequence. A
fenfible governefs cannot attend to the
                                    minds

minds of the number she is obliged to
have.   She may have been many years
struggling to get established, and when
fortune smiles, does not chuse to lose
the opportunity of providing for old
age; therefore continues to enlarge her
school, with a view to accumulate a
competency for that purpose.   Domestic concerns cannot possibly be
made a part of their employment, or
proper conversations often entered on.
Improper books will by stealth be in-
troduced, and the bad example of
one or two vicious children, in the
play-hours, infect a number.   Their
gratitude and tenderness are not called
forth in the way they might be by
                                    maternal

maternal affection. Many miseries does
a girl of a mild disposition suffer, which
a tender parent could guard her from.
I shall not contest about the graces,
but the virtues are best learnt at home,
if a mother will give up her time and
thoughts to the task ; but if she cannot, they should be sent to school ; for
people who do not manage their children well, and have not large fortunes,
must leave them often with servants,
where they are in danger of still greater
corruptions.

THE

The TEMPER.

THE forming of the temper ought to be the continual thought, and the firſt taſk of a parent or teacher. For to ſpeak moderately, half the miſeries of life ariſe from peeviſhneſs, or a tyrannical domineering temper. The tender, who are ſo by nature, or thoſe whom religion has moulded with ſo heavenly a diſpoſition, give way for the ſake of peace—yet ſtill this giving way undermines their domeſtic comfort, and ſtops the current of affection; they labor for patience, and labor is ever painful.

The

The governing of our temper is truly the bufinefs of our whole lives; but furely it would very much affift us if we were early put into the right road. As it is, when reafon gains fome ftrength, fhe has mountains of rubbifh to remove, or perhaps exerts all her powers to juftify the errors of folly and paffion, rather than root them out.

A conftant attention to the manage-ment of the temper produces gentle-nefs and humility, and is practifed on all occafions, as it is not done " to be feen of men." This meek fpirit arifes from good fenfe and refolution, and fhould not be confounded with indo-

lence

lence and timidity; weakneſſes of mind,
which often paſs for good nature. She
who ſubmits, without conviction, to a
parent or huſband, will as unreaſon-
ably tyranniſe over her ſervants; for
ſlaviſh fear and tyranny go together.
Reſentment, indeed, may and will be
felt occaſionally by the beſt of human
beings; yet humility will ſoon conquer it, and convert ſcorn and contempt into pity, and drive out that
haſty pride which is always guarding
Self from inſult; which takes fire on the
moſt trivial occaſions, and which will not
admit of a ſuperior, or even an equal.
With ſuch a temper is often joined
that baſhful aukwardneſs which ariſes
                                    from

from ignorance, and is frequently termed diffidence; but which does not, in
my opinion, deferve fuch a diftinction.
True humility is not innate, but like
every other good quality muft be cultivated. Reflections on mifcarriages
of conduct, and miftakes in opinion,
fink it deep into the mind; efpecially
if thofe mifcarriages and miftakes have
been a caufe of pain—when we fmart
for our folly we remember it.

Few people look into their own
hearts, or think of their tempers,
though they feverely cenfure others,
on whofe fide they fay the fault always
lies. Now I am apt to believe, that
there

there is not a temper in the world
which does not need correction, and
of courfe attention. Thofe who are
termed good-humored, are frequently giddy, indolent, and infenfible; yet
becaufe the fociety they mix with appear feldom difpleafed with a perfon
who does not conteft, and will laugh
off an affront, they imagine themfelves
pleafing, when they are only not difagreeable. Warm tempers are too
eafily irritated. The one requires a
fpur, the other a rein. Health of
mind, as well as body, muft in general
be obtained by patient fubmiffion to
felf-denial, and difagreeable opera-
tions.

F   If

If the presence of the Deity be inculcated and dwelt on till an habitual
reverence is established in the mind,
it will check the sallies of anger and
sneers of peevishness, which corrode
our peace, and render us wretched,
without any claim to pity.

The wisdom of the Almighty has
so ordered things, that one cause produces many effects. While we are
looking into another's mind, and forming their temper, we are insensibly
correcting our own; and every act
of benevolence which we exert to our
fellow-creatures, does ourselves the
most essential services. Active virtue

fits

fits us for the fociety of more exalted beings. Our philanthrophy is a proof, we are told, that we are capable of loving our Creator. Indeed this divine love, or charity, appears to me the principal trait that remains of the illuf-trious image of the Deity, which was originally ftampt on the foul, and which is to be renewed. Exalted views will raife the mind above trifling cares, and the many little weakneffes, which make us a torment to ourfelves and others. Our temper will gradu-ally improve, and vanity, which " the creature is made fubject to," has not an entire dominion.

F 2   But

But I have digreffed.   A judicious parent can only manage a child in this important article; and example will beft enforce precept.

Be careful, however, not to make hypocrites; fmothered flames will blaze out with more violence for hav- ing been kept down.   Expect not to do all yourfelf; experience muft enable the child to affift you; you can only lay the foundation, or prevent bad propenfities from fettling into habits.

U n-

UNFORTUNATE SITUATION OF FE-
MALES, FASHIONABLY EDUCATED,
AND LEFT WITHOUT A FORTUNE.

I HAVE hitherto only fpoken of thofe females, who will have a provifion made for them by their parents. But many who have been well, or at leaft fafhionably educated, are left without a fortune, and if they are not entirely devoid of delicacy, they muft frequently remain fingle.

Few are the modes of earning a fubfiftence, and thofe very humiliating. Perhaps to be an humble companion to fome rich old coufin, or what is ftill

F 3 worfe,

worfe, to live with ftrangers, who are
fo intolerably tyrannical, that none of
their own relations can bear to live
with them, though they fhould even
expect a fortune in reverfion. It is
impoffible to enumerate the many
hours of anguifh fuch a perfon muft
fpend. Above the fervants, yet confidered by them as a fpy, and ever reminded of her inferiority when in
converfation with the fuperiors. If
fhe cannot condefcend to mean flat-
tery, fhe has not a chance of being a
favorite; and fhould any of the vi-
fitors take notice of her, and fhe for a
moment forget her fubordinate ftate,
fhe is fure to be reminded of it.

Pain-

Painfully senfible of unkindnefs, fhe is alive to every thing, and many far-cafms reach her, which were perhaps directed another way. She is alone, fhut out from equality and confidence, and the concealed anxiety impairs her conftitution; for fhe muft wear a cheerful face, or be difmiffed. The being dependant on the caprice of a fellow-creature, though certainly very neceffary in this ftate of difcipline, is yet a very bitter corrective, which we would fain fhrink from.

A teacher at a fchool is only a kind of upper fervant, who has more work than the menial ones.

F 4

A go-

A governess to young ladies is equally difagreeable. It is ten to one if they meet with a reafonable mother; and if fhe is not fo, fhe will be continually finding fault to prove fhe is not ignorant, and be difpleafed if her pupils do not improve, but angry if the proper methods are taken to make them do fo. The children treat them with difrefpect, and often with infolence. In the mean time life glides away, and the fpirits with it; " and when youth and genial years are flown," they have nothing to fubfift on; or, perhaps, on fome extraordinary occafion, fome fmall allowance may be made for them, which is thought a great charity.

The

The few trades which are left, are now gradually falling into the hands of the men, and certainly they are not very respectable.

It is hard for a person who has a relish for polished society, to herd with the vulgar, or to condescend to mix with her former equals when she is considered in a different light. What unwelcome heart-breaking knowledge is then poured in on her! I mean a view of the selfishness and depravity of the world; for every other acquirement is a source of pleasure, though they may occasion temporary inconveniences. How cutting is the con-

tempt

tempt she meets with!—A young mind looks round for love and friendship; but love and friendship fly from poverty: expect them not if you are poor! The mind must then sink into meanness, and accommodate itself to its new state, or dare to be unhappy. Yet I think no reflecting person would give up the experience and improvement they have gained, to have avoided the misfortunes; on the contrary, they are thankfully ranked amongst the choicest blessings of life, when we are not under their immediate pressure.

How earnestly does a mind full of sensibility look for disinterested friendship,

2

ship, and long to meet with good un-
alloyed. When fortune smiles they
hug the dear delusion; but dream not
that it is one. The painted cloud dis-
appears suddenly, the scene is chang-
ed, and what an aching void is left in
the heart! a void which only religion
can fill up—and how few seek this
internal comfort!

A woman, who has beauty without
sentiment, is in great danger of being
seduced; and if she has any, cannot
guard herself from painful mortifica-
tions. It is very disagreeable to keep
up a continual reserve with men she
has been formerly familiar with; yet
if

if she places confidence, it is ten to one but she is deceived. Few men seriously think of marrying an inferior; and if they have honor enough not to take advantage of the artless tenderness of a woman who loves, and thinks not of the difference of rank, they do not undeceive her until she has anticipated happiness, which, contrasted with her dependant situation, appears delightful. The disappointment is severe; and the heart receives a wound which does not easily admit of a compleat cure, as the good that is missed is not valued according to its real worth: for fancy drew the picture, and grief delights to create food to feed on.

If

If what I have written should be read by parents, who are now going on in thoughtless extravagance, and anxious only that their daughters may be *genteelly educated*, let them consider to what sorrows they expose them ; for I have not over-coloured the picture.

Though I warn parents to guard against leaving their daughters to encounter so much misery ; yet if a young woman falls into it, she ought not to be discontented. Good must ultimately arise from every thing, to those who look beyond this infancy of their being ; and here the comfort of a good conscience is our only stable support. The main business of our lives is to

learn

learn to be virtuous; and He who is training us up for immortal blifs, knows beſt what trials will contribute to make us ſo; and our reſignation and improvement will render us reſpectable to ourſelves, and to that Being, whoſe approbation is of more value than life itſelf. It is true, tribulation produces anguiſh, and we would fain avoid the bitter cup, though convinced its effects would be the moſt ſalutary. The Almighty is then the kind parent, who chaſtens and educates, and indulges us not when it would tend to our hurt. He is compaſſion itſelf, and never wounds but to heal, when the ends of correction are anſwered.

LOVE.

L O V E.

I THINK there is not a subject that admits so little of reasoning on as love; nor can rules be laid down that will not appear to lean too much one way or the other. Circumstances must, in a great measure, govern the conduct in this particular; yet who can be a judge in their own case? Perhaps, before they begin to consider the matter, they see through the medium of passion, and its suggestions are often mistaken for those of reason. We can no other way account for the absurd matches we every day have an opportunity of observing; for in this

respect,

respect, even the most sensible men and women err. A variety of causes will occasion an attachment; an endeavour to supplant another, or being by some accident confined to the society of one person. Many have found themselves entangled in an affair of honor, who only meant to fill up the heavy hours in an amusing way, or raise jealousy in some other bosom.

It is a difficult task to write on a subject when our own passions are likely to blind us. Hurried away by our feelings, we are apt to set those things down as general maxims, which only our partial experience gives rise to.

to. Though it is not eafy to fay how a perfon fhould act under the immediate influence of paffion, yet they certainly have no excufe who are actuated only by vanity, and deceive by an equivocal behaviour in order to gratify it. There are quite as many male coquets as female, and they are far more pernicious pefts to fociety, as their fphere of action is larger, and they are lefs expofed to the cenfure of the world. A fmothered figh, down-caft look, and the many other little arts which are played off, may give extreme pain to a fincere, artlefs woman, though fhe cannot refent, or complain

G of

of, the injury. This kind of trifling, I think, much more inexcusable than inconstancy; and why it is so, appears so obvious, I need not point it out.

People of sense and reflection are most apt to have violent and constant passions, and to be preyed on by them. Neither can they, for the sake of present pleasure, bear to act in such a manner, as that the retrospect should fill them with confusion and regret. Perhaps a delicate mind is not susceptible of a greater degree of misery, putting guilt out of the question, than what must arise from the consciousness

of

of loving a perſon whom their reaſon does not approve. This, I am perſuaded, has often been the caſe ; and the paſſion muſt either be rooted out, or the continual allowances and excuſes that are made will hurt the mind, and leſſen the reſpect for virtue. Love, unſupported by eſteem, muſt ſoon expire, or lead to depravity ; as, on the contrary, when a worthy perſon is the object, it is the greateſt incentive to improvement, and has the beſt effect on the manners and temper. We ſhould always try to fix in our minds the rational grounds we have for loving a perſon, that we may be able to recollect them when we feel diſguſt or re-

ſent-

fentment; we fhould then habitually
practife forbearance, and the many
petty difputes which interrupt domeftic
peace would be avoided. A woman
cannot reafonably be unhappy, if fhe
is attached to a man of fenfe and
goodnefs, though he may not be all
fhe could wifh.

I am very far from thinking love
irrefiftible, and not to be conquered.
" If weak women go aftray," it is
they, and not the ftars, that are to be
blamed. A refolute endeavour will
almoft always overcome difficulties.
I knew a woman very early in life
warmly attached to an agreeable man,

yet fhe faw his faults; his principles were unfixed, and his prodigal turn would have obliged her to have re-ftrained every benevolent emotion of her heart. She exerted her influence to improve him, but in vain did fhe for years try to do it. Convinced of the impoffibility, fhe determined not to marry him, though fhe was forced to encounter poverty and its attendants.

It is too univerfal a maxim with novelifts, that love is felt but once; though it appears to me, that the heart which is capable of receiving an im-preffion at all, and can diftinguifh, will turn to a new object when the firft is

G 3   found

found unworthy. I am convinced it is practicable, when a refpect for goodnefs has the firft place in the mind, and notions of perfection are not affixed to conftancy. Many ladies are delicately miferable, and imagine that they are lamenting the lofs of a lover, when they are full of felf-applaufe, and reflections on their own fuperior refinement. Painful feelings are prolonged beyond their natural courfe, to gratify our defire of appearing heroines, and we deceive ourfelves as well as others. When any fudden ftroke of fate deprives us of thofe we love, we may not readily get the better of the blow; but when we find we have

been

been led aftray by our paffions, and
that it was our own imaginations
which gave the high colouring to the
picture, we may be certain time will
drive it out of our minds. For we
cannot often think of our folly without being difpleafed with ourfelves,
and fuch reflections are quickly ba-
nifhed. Habit and duty will co-operate, and religion may overcome what
reafon has in vain combated with;
but refinement and romance are often
confounded, and fenfibility, which occafions this kind of inconftancy, is
fuppofed to have the contrary effect.

G 4

No-

Nothing can more tend to destroy peace of mind, than platonic attachments. They are begun in false refinement, and frequently end in sorrow, if not in guilt. The two extremes often meet, and virtue carried to excess will sometimes lead to the opposite vice. Not that I mean to insinuate that there is no such thing as friendship between persons of different sexes; I am convinced of the contrary. I only mean to observe, that if a woman's heart is disengaged, she should not give way to a pleasing delusion, and imagine she will be satisfied with the friendship of a man she admires, and prefers to the rest of the world.

The

The heart is very treacherous, and if we do not guard its firſt emotions, we ſhall not afterwards be able to prevent its ſighing for impoſſibilities. If there are any inſuperable bars to an union in the common way, try to diſmiſs the dangerous tenderneſs, or it will undermine your comfort, and betray you into many errors. To attempt to raiſe ourſelves above human beings is ridiculous; we cannot extirpate our paſſions, nor is it neceſſary that we ſhould, though it may be wiſe ſometimes not to ſtray too near a precipice, leſt we fall over before we are aware. We cannot avoid much vexation and ſorrow, if we are ever ſo prudent; it is then

the

the part of wifdom to enjoy thofe
gleams of funfhine which do not en-
danger our innocence, or lead to repentance. Love gilds all the profpects
of life, and though it cannot always
exclude apathy, it makes many cares
appear trifling. Dean Swift hated the
world, and only loved particular perfons; yet pride rivalled them. A
foolifh wifh of rifing fuperior to the
common wants and defires of the
human fpecies made him fingular, but
not refpectable. He facrificed an amiable woman to his caprice, and made
thofe fhun his company who would
have been entertained and improved
by his converfation, had he loved any
                                    one

one as well as himself. Univerſal benevolence is the firſt duty, and we
ſhould be careful not to let any paſſion ſo engroſs our thoughts, as to prevent our practiſing it. After all the
dreams of rapture, earthly pleaſures
will not fill the mind, or ſupport it
when they have not the ſanction of
reaſon, or are too much depended on.
The tumult of paſſion will ſubſide,
and even the pangs of diſappointment
ment ceaſe to be felt. But for the
wicked there is a worm that never
dies—a guilty conſcience. While that
calm ſatisfaction which reſignation
produces, which cannot be deſcribed,

but

but may be attained, in fome degree, by thofe who try to keep in the ftrait, though thorny path which leads to blifs, fhall fanctify the forrows, and dignify the character of virtue.

MATRI-

MATRIMONY.

EARLY marriages are, in my opinion, a ſtop to improvement. If we were born only " to draw nutrition, propagate and rot," the ſooner the end of creation was anſwered the better; but as women are here allowed to have ſouls, the ſoul ought to be attended to. In youth a woman endeavours to pleaſe the other ſex, in order, generally ſpeaking, to get married, and this endeavour calls forth all her powers. If ſhe has had a tolerable education, the foundation only is laid, for the mind does not ſoon arrive at maturity, and ſhould not be en-
groſſed

groffed by domeſtic cares before any habits are fixed. The paſſions alſo have too much influence over the judgment to ſuffer it to direct her in this moſt important affair; and many women, I am perſuaded, marry a man before they are twenty, whom they would have rejected ſome years after. Very frequently, when the education has been neglected, the mind improves itſelf, if it has leiſure for reflection, and experience to reflect on; but how can this happen when they are forced to act before they have had time to think, or find that they are unhappily married? Nay, ſhould they be ſo fortunate as to get a good huſband, they

will

will not fet a proper value on him; he
will be found much inferior to the
lovers defcribed in novels, and their
want of knowledge makes them frequently difgufted with the man, when
the fault is in human nature.

When a woman's mind has gained
fome ftrength, fhe will in all probabi-
lity pay more attention to her actions
than a girl can be expected to do;
and if fhe thinks ferioufly, fhe will
chufe for a companion a man of principle; and this perhaps young people
do not fufficiently attend to, or fee
the neceffity of doing. A woman of
feeling muft be very much hurt if fhe

is

is obliged to keep her children out of their father's company, that their morals may not be injured by his converfation; and befides, the whole arduous tafk of education devolves on her, and in fuch a cafe it is not very practicable. Attention to the education of children muft be irkfome, when life appears to have fo many charms, and its pleafures are not found fallacious. Many are but juft returned from a boarding-fchool, when they are placed at the head of a family, and how fit they are to manage it, I leave the judicious to judge. Can they improve a child's underftanding, when they are fcarcely out of the ftate of childhood themfelves?

Dignity

Dignity of manners, too, and proper reserve are often wanting. The conftant attendant on too much familiarity is contempt. Women are often before marriage prudifh, and afterwards they think they may innocently give way to fondnefs, and overwhelm the poor man with it. They think they have a legal right to his affections, and grow remifs in their endeavours to pleafe. There are a thoufand name-lefs decencies which good fenfe gives rife to, and artlefs proofs of regard which flow from the heart, and will reach it, if it is not depraved. It has ever occurred to me, that is was fuf-ficient for a woman to receive careffes,

H   and

and not beftow them. She ought to diftinguifh between fondnefs and tendernefs. The latter is the fweeteft cordial of life ; but, like all other cordials, fhould be referved for particular occafions ; to exhilarate the fpirits, when depreffed by ficknefs, or loft in forrow. Senfibility will beft inftruct. Some delicacies can never be pointed out or defcribed, though they fink deep into the heart, and render the hours of diftrefs fupportable.

A woman fhould have fo proper a pride, as not eafily to forget a deliberate affront ; though fhe muft not too haftily refent any little coolnefs. We

3

We cannot always feel alike, and all are fubject to changes of temper without an adequate caufe.

Reafon muft often be called in to fill up the vacuums of life; but too many of our fex fuffer theirs to lie dormant. A little ridicule and fmart turn of expreffion, often confutes without convincing; and tricks are played off to raife tendernefs, even while they are forfeiting efteem.

Women are faid to be the weaker veffel, and many are the miferies which this weaknefs brings on them. Men have in fome refpects very much the ad-

H 2   vantage.

vantage. If they have a tolerable underftanding, it has a chance to be cultivated. They are forced to fee human nature as it is, and are not left to
dwell on the pictures of their own imaginations. Nothing, I am fure, calls
forth the faculties fo much as the being obliged to ftruggle with the world ;
and this is not a woman's province in
a married ftate. Her fphere of action
is not large, and if fhe is not taught to
look into her own heart, how trivial
are her occupations and purfuits !
What little arts engrofs and narrow
her mind ! " Cunning fills up the
mighty void of fenfe ;" and cares,
which do not improve the heart or un
                              derftand

derstanding, take up her attention. Of course, she falls a prey to childish anger, and silly capricious humors, which render her rather insignificant than vicious.

In a comfortable situation, a cultivated mind is necessary to render a woman contented ; and in a miserable one, it is her only consolation. A sensible, delicate woman, who by some strange accident, or mistake, is joined to a fool or a brute, must be wretched beyond all names of wretchedness, if her views are confined to the present scene. Of what importance, then, is intellectual improvement, when our

H 3   com-

comfort here, and happiness hereafter,
depends upon it.

Principles of religion should be fixed, and the mind not left to fluctuate
in the time of distress, when it can receive succour from no other quarter.
The conviction that every thing is
working for our good will scarcely
produce resignation, when we are deprived of our dearest hopes. How
they can be satisfied, who have not
this conviction, I cannot conceive ; I
rather think they will turn to some
worldly support, and fall into folly, if
not vice.   For a little refinement only
leads a woman into the wilds of romance,

mance, if she is not religious; nay, more, there is no true sentiment without it, nor perhaps any other effectual check to the passions.

DE.

DESULTORY THOUGHTS.

AS every kind of domeſtic concern and family buſineſs is properly a woman's province, to enable her to diſcharge her duty ſhe ſhould ſtudy the different branches of it. Nothing is more uſeful in a family than a little knowledge of phyſic, ſufficient to make the miſtreſs of it a judicious nurſe. Many a perſon, who has had a ſenſible phyſician to attend them, have been loſt for want of the other; for tenderneſs, without judgment, ſometimes does more harm than good.

The ignorant imagine there is ſomething very myſterious in the practice

of

of phyſic. They expect a medicine to work like a charm, and know no-thing of the progreſs and criſis of diſ-orders. The keeping of the patient low appears cruel, all kind of regimen is diſregarded, and though the fever rages, they cannot be perſuaded not to give them inflammatory food. " How (ſay they) can a perſon get well without nouriſhment ?"

The mind, too, ſhould be ſoothed at the ſame time ; and indeed, when-ever it ſinks, ſoothing is, at firſt, better than reaſoning. The ſlackened nerves are not to be braced by words. When a mind is worried by care, or oppreſſed

by

by forrow, it cannot in a moment
grow tranquil, and attend to the voice
of reafon.

St. Paul fays, " No chaftening for
the prefent feemeth to be joyous ; but
grievous : neverthelefs, afterwards it
yieldeth the peaceable fruits of righte-
oufnefs unto them which are exercifed
thereby." It is plain, from thefe
words of the Apoftle, and from many
other parts of Scripture, that afflictions are neceffary to teach us true
wifdom, and that in fpite of this conviction, men would fain avoid the
bitter draught, though certain that the
drinking of it would be conducive to
the

the purifying of their hearts. He who made us muſt know what will tend to our ultimate good; yet ſtill all this is grievous, and the heart will throb with anguiſh when deprived of what it loves, and the tongue can ſcarcely faulter out an acquieſcence to the Divine Will, when it is ſo contrary to our own. Due allowance ought then to be made for human infirmities, and the unhappy ſhould be conſidered as objects of com-paſſion, rather than blame. But in a very different ſtile does conſolatory advice generally run; for inſtead of pouring oil or wine into the wound, it tends to convince the unfortunate perſons that they are weak as well as unhappy.

I am

I am apt to imagine, that sorrow and resignation are not incompatible ; and that though religion cannot make some disappointments pleasant, it prevents our repining, even while we smart under them. Did our feelings and reason always coincide, our passage through this world could not justly be termed a warfare, and faith would no longer be a virtue. It is our preferring the things that are not seen, to those which are, that proves us to be the heirs of promise.

On the sacred word of the Most High, we rely with firm assurance, that the sufferings of the present life will

will work out a far more exceeding
and eternal weight of glory; yet ftill
they are allowed to be afflictions,
which, though temporary, muft ftill
be grievous.

The difference between thofe who
forrow without hope, and thofe who
look up to Heaven, is not that the
one feel more than the other, for they
may be both equally depreffed; but
the latter think of the peaceable fruits
which are to refult from the difcipline, and therefore patiently fubmit.

I have almoft run into a fermon,—
and I fhall not make an apology for it.
What-

Whatever contributes to make us compassionate and resolute, is of the utmost consequence; both these qualities are necessary, if we are confined to a sick chamber. Various are the misfortunes of life, and it may be the lot of most of us to see death in all its terrors, when it attacks a friend; yet even then we must exert our friend-ship, and try to chear the departing spirit.

THE

THE BENEFITS WHICH ARISE FROM DISAPPOINMENTS.

MOST women, and men too, have no character at all. Juft opinions and virtuous paffions appear by ftarts, and while we are giving way to the love and admiration which thofe qualities raife, they are quite different creatures. It is reflection which forms habits, and fixes principles indelibly on the heart; without it, the mind is like a wreck drifted about by every fquall. The paffion that we think moft of will foon rival all the reft; it is then in our power, this way, to ftrengthen our

good

good difpofitions, and in fome meafure
to eftablifh a character, which will not
depend on every accidental impulfe.
To be convinced of truths, and yet
not to feel or act up to them, is a
common thing. Prefent pleafure drives
all before it, and adverfity is merci-
fully fent to force us to think.

In the fchool of adverfity we learn
knowledge as well as virtue; yet we
lament our hard fate, dwell on our dif-
appointments, and never confider that
our own wayward minds, and incon-
fiftent hearts, require thefe needful
correctives. Medicines are not fent
to perfons in health.

It

It is a well-known remark, that our very wishes give us not our wish. I have often thought it might be set down as a maxim, that the greatest disappointment we can meet with is the gratification of our fondest wishes. But truth is sometimes not pleasant; we turn from it, and doat on an illusion; and if we were not in a probationary state, we should do well to thicken the cloud, rather than dispel it.

There are some who delight in observing moral beauty, and their souls sicken when forced to view crimes and follies which could never hurt them. How numerous are the sorrows which

I   reach

reach fuch bofoms! They may truly
be called *human creatures*; on every
fide they touch their fellow-mortals,
and vibrate to the touch. Common
humanity points out the important duties of our ftation; but fenfibility (a
kind of inftinct, ftrengthened by reflection) can only teach the numberlefs
minute things which give pain or
pleafure.

A benevolent mind often fuffers
more than the object it commiferates,
and will bear an inconvenience itfelf
to fhelter another from it. It makes
allowance for failings though it longs
to meet perfection, which it feems
formed

formed to adore. The Author of all good continually calls himfelf, a God long-fuffering; and thofe moft refemble him who practife forbearance. Love and compaffion are the moft delightful feelings of the foul, and to exert them to all that breathe is the wifh of the benevolent heart. To ftruggle with ingratitude and felfifhnefs is grating beyond expreffion: and the fenfe we have of our weaknefs, though ufeful, is not pleafant. Thus it is with us, when we look for happinefs, we meet with vexations: and if, now and then, we give way to tendernefs, or any of the amiable paffions, and tafte pleafure, the mind, ftrained beyond its

I 2 ufual

ufual tone, falls into apathy.   And yet
we were made to be happy! But our
paffions will not contribute much to
our blifs, till they are under the dominion of reafon, and till that reafon
is enlightened and improved.   Then
fighing will ceafe, and all tears will be
wiped away by that Being, in whofe
prefence there is fulnefs of joy.

A perfon of tendernefs muft ever
have particular attachments, and ever
be difappointed; yet ftill they muft be
attached, in fpite of human frailty;
for if the mind is not kept in motion
by either hope or fear, it finks into
the dreadful ftate before-mentioned.

I have

I have very often heard it made a subject of ridicule, that when a person is disappointed in this world, they turn to the next. Nothing can be more natural than the transition; and it seems to me the scheme of Providence, that our finding things unsatisfactory here, should force us to think of the better country to which we are going.

I 3   ON

ON THE TREATMENT OF
SERVANTS.

THE management of servants is a great part of the employment of a woman's life; and her own temper depends very much on her behaviour to them.

Servants are, in general, ignorant and cunning; we must consider their characters, if we would treat them properly, and continually practise forbearance. The same methods we use with children may be adopted with regard to them. Act uniformly, and never find fault without a just cause;
and

and when there is, be positive, but not
angry. A mind that is not too much
engrossed by trifles, will not be discom-
posed by every little domestic disaster ;
and a thinking person can very readily
make allowance for those faults which
arise from want of reflection and education. I have seen the peace of a
whole family disturbed by some trivial,
cross accident, and hours spent in use-
less upbraidings about some mistake
which would never have been thought
of, but for the consequences that arose
from it. An error in judgment or an
accident should not be severely repre-
hended. It is a proof of wisdom to

I 4 profit

profit by experience, and not lament irremediable evils.

A benevolent perfon muſt ever wiſh to ſee thoſe around them comfortable, and try to be the cauſe of that comfort. The wide difference which education makes, I ſhould ſuppoſe, would prevent familiarity in the way of equality; yet kindneſs muſt be ſhewn, if we are deſirous that our domeſtics ſhould be attached to our intereſt and perſons. How pleaſing it is to be attended with a ſmile of willingneſs, to be conſulted when they are at a loſs, and looked up to as a friend and benefactor when they are in diſtreſs. It

3   is

is true we may often meet with ingratitude, but it ought not to difcourage
us; the refrefhing fhowers of heaven
fertilize the fields of the unworthy, as
well as the juft. We fhould nurfe
them in illnefs, and our fuperior judgment in thofe matters would often alleviate their pains.

Above all, we owe them a good
example. The ceremonials of religion, on their account, fhould be attended to; as they always reverence
them to a fuperftitious degree, or elfe
negleét them. We fhould not fhock
the faith of the meaneft fellow-creature; nay more, we fhould comply
with

with their prejudices; for their religious notions are fo over-run with
them, that they are not eafily feparat-
ed; and by trying to pluck up the
tares, we may root up the wheat with
them.

The woman who gives way to caprice and ill-humour in the kitchen,
cannot eafily fmooth her brow when
her hufband returns to his fire-fide;
nay, he may not only fee the wrinkles
of anger, but hear the difputes at
fecond-hand. I heard a Gentleman
fay, it would break any man's heart to
hear his wife argue fuch a cafe. Men
who are employed about things of
confe-

confequence, think thefe affairs more infignificant than they really are; for the warmth with which we engage in any bufinefs increafes its importance, and our not entering into them has the contrary effect.

The behaviour of girls to fervants is generally in extremes; too familiar or haughty. Indeed the one often produces the other, as a check, when the freedoms are troublefome.

We cannot make our fervants wife or good, but we may teach them to be decent and orderly; and order leads to fome degree of morality.

THE

THE OBSERVANCE OF SUNDAY.

THE inftitution of keeping the feventh day holy was wifely ordered by Providence for two purpofes. To reft the body, and call off the mind from the too eager purfuit of the fhadows of this life, which, I am afraid, often obfcure the profpect of futurity, and fix our thoughts on earth. A refpect for this ordinance is, I am perfuaded, of the utmoft confequence to national religion. The vulgar have fuch a notion of it, that with them, going to church, and being religious, are almoft fynonymous terms. They

are

are fo loft in their fenfes, that if this
day did not continually remind them,
they would foon forget that there was
a God in the world. Some forms are
neceffary to fupport vital religion, and
without them it would foon languifh,
and at laft expire.

It is unfortunate, that this day is
either kept with puritanical exactnefs,
which renders it very irkfome, or loft
in diffipation and thoughtleffnefs. Either way is very prejudicial to the
minds of children and fervants, who
ought not to be let run wild, nor
confined too ftrictly; and, above all,
fhould not fee their parents or mafters
indulge

indulge themselves in things which
are generally thought wrong. I am
fully perfuaded, that fervants have fuch
a notion of card-playing, that where-
ever it is practifed of a Sunday their
minds are hurt; and the barrier between good and evil in fome meafure
broken down.   Servants, who are accuftomed to bodily labour, will fall
into as laborious pleafures, if they are
not gently reftrained, and fome fub-
ftitute found out for them.

Such a clofe attention to a family
may appear to many very difagreeable; but the path of duty will be
found pleafant after fome time; and
the

the paffions being employed this way, will, by degrees, come under the fub-jection of reafon. I mean not to be rigid, the obftructions which arife in the way of our duty, do not ftrike a fpeculatift; I know, too, that in the moment of action, even a well-difpofed mind is often carried away by the prefent impulfe, and that it requires fome experience to be able to diftin-guifh the dictates of reafon from thofe of paffion. The truth is feldom found out until the tumult is over; we then wake as from a dream, and when we furvey what we have done, and feel the folly of it, we might call on rea-fon and fay, why fleepeft thou? Yet

though

though people are led astray by their passions, and even relapse after the most bitter repentance, they should not despair, but still try to regain the right road, and cultivate such habits as may assist them.

I never knew much social virtue to reside in a house where the sabbath was grossly violated.

ON

ON THE MISFORTUNE OF
FLUCTUATING PRINCIPLES.

IF we look for any comfort in friendship or society, we muſt aſſociate
with thoſe who have fixed principles
with reſpect to religion ; for without
them, repeated experience convinces
me, the moſt ſhining qualities are un-
ſtable, and not to be depended on.

It has often been a matter of ſur-
priſe to me, that ſo few people examine the tenets of the religion they
profeſs, or are chriſtians through conviction. They have no anchor to reſt
on, nor any fixed chart to direct them

K   in

in the doubtful voyage of life; how then can they hope to find the " haven of reft ?" But they think not of it, and cannot be expected to forego prefent advantages. Noble actions muft arife from noble thoughts and views ; when they are confined to this world, they muft be groveling.

Faith, with refpect to the promife of eternal happinefs, can only enable us to combat with our paffions, with a chance of victory. There are many who pay no attention to revelation, and more, perhaps, who have not any fixed belief in it. The fure word of comfott is neglected ; and how people

3   can

can live without it, I can scarcely
conceive. For as the sun renews the
face of nature, and chases away dark-
ness from the world, so does this, still
greater blessing, have the same effect
on the mind, and enlightens and cheers
it when every thing else fails.

A true sense of our infirmities is the
way to make us christians in the most
extensive sense of the word. A mind
depressed with a weight of weaknesses
can only find comfort in the promises
of the Gospel. The assistance there
offered must raise the humble soul;
and the account of the atonement
that has been made, gives a rational

ground

ground for refting in hope until the
toil of virtue is over, and faith has
nothing to be exercifed on.

It is the fafhion now for young men
to be deifts.   And many a one has
improper books fent adrift in a fea
of doubts—of which there is no end.
This is not a land of certainty ; there
is no confining the wandering reafon, and but one clue to prevent its
being loft in endlefs refearches.   Reafon is indeed the heaven-lighted lamp
in man, and may fafely be trufted
when not entirely depended on ; but
when it pretends to difcover what is
beyond its ken, it certainly ftretches
the

the line too far, and runs into abfur-
dity. Some fpeculations are idle and
others hurtful, as they raife pride, and
turn the thoughts to fubjects that
ought to be left unexplored. With
love and awe we fhould think of the
High and Lofty One, that inhabiteth
eternity! and not prefume to fay how
He muft exift who created us. How
unfortunate it is, that man muft fink
into a brute, and not employ his mind,
or elfe, by thinking, grow fo proud,
as often to imagine himfelf a fuperior being! It is not the doubts of
profound thinkers that I here allude
to, but the crude notions which young
men fport away when together, and

fome-

fometimes in the company of young women, to make them wonder at their fuperior wifdom! There cannot be any thing more dangerous to a mind, not accuftomed to think, than doubts delivered in a ridiculing way. They never go deep enough to folve them, of courfe they ftick by them; and though they might not influence their conduct, if a fear of the world prevents their being guilty of vices, yet their thoughts are not reftrained, and they fhould be obferved diligently, " For out of them are the iffues of life." A nice fenfe of right and wrong ought to be acquired, and then not only great vices will be avoided, but every little meannefs; truth will reign

in

in the inward parts, and mercy will attend her.

I have indeed so much compassion for those young females who are entering into the world without fixed principles, that I would fain persuade them to examine a little into the matter. For though in the season of gaiety they may not feel the want of them, in that of distress where will they fly for succour? Even with this support, life is a labor of patience—a conflict; and the utmost we can gain is a small portion of peace, a kind of watchful tranquillity, that is liable to continual interruptions.

K 4

" Then

" Then keep each paffion down, however dear;

" Truft me, the tender are the moft fevere.

" Guard, while 'tis thine, thy philofophic eafe,

" And afk no joy but that of virtuous peace;

" That bids defiance to the ftorms of fate:

" High blifs is only for a higher ftate."

THOMSON.

BENE-

BENEVOLENCE.

THIS first, and most amiable virtue, is often found in young
persons that afterwards grow selfish;
a knowledge of the arts of others, is
an excuse to them for practising the
same; and because they have been
deceived once, or have found objects
unworthy of their charity—if any one
appeals to their feelings, the formida-
ble word Imposture instantly banishes
the compassionate emotions, and si-
lences conscience. I do not mean to
confine the exercise of benevolence to
alms-giving, though it is a very mate-
rial part of it. Faith, hope, and cha-

2   rity,

rity, ought to attend us in our paſſage through this world; but the two firſt leave us when we die, while the other is to be the conſtant inmate of our breaſt through all eternity. We ought not to ſuffer the heavenly ſpark to be quenched by ſelfiſhneſs; if we do, how can we expect it to revive, when the ſoul is diſentangled from the body, and ſhould be prepared for the realms of love? Forbearance and liberality of ſentiment are the virtues of maturity. Children ſhould be taught every thing in a poſitive way; and their own experience can only teach them afterwards to make diſtinctions and allowances. It is then the inferior part of

bene-

benevolence that comes within their
fphere of action, and it fhould not be
fuffered to fleep. Some part of the
money that is allowed them for pocket-
money, they fhould be encouraged to
lay out this way, and the fhort-lived
emotions of pity continually retraced
'till they grow into habits.

I knew a child that would, when
very young, fit down and cry if it met
a poor perfon, after it had laid out its
money in cakes; this occurred once
or twice, and the tears were fhed with
additional diftrefs every time; till at
laft it refifted the temptation, and
faved the money.

I think

I think it a very good method for girls to have a certain allowance for cloaths. A mother can eafily, without feeming to do it, obferve how they fpend it, and direct them accordingly. By thefe means they would learn the value of money, and be obliged to contrive. This would be a practical leffon of œconomy fuperior to all the theories that could be thought of. The having a fixed ftipend, too, would enable them to be charitable, in the true fenfe of the word, as they would then give their own ; and by denying themfelves little ornaments, and doing their own work, they might increafe the fum appropriated to charitable purpofes.

A lively

A lively principle of this kind would
alſo overcome indolence ; for I have
known people waſteful and penurious
at the ſame time ; but the waſteful-
neſs was to ſpare themſelves trouble,
and others only felt the effects of their
penury, to make the balance even.

Women too often confine their love
and charity to their own families.
They fix not in their minds the prece-
dency of moral obligations, or make
their feelings give way to duty. Good-
will to all the human race ſhould dwell
in our boſoms, nor ſhould love to in-
dividuals induce us to violate this firſt
of duties, or make us ſacrifice the intereſt

tereft of any fellow-creature, to pro-
mote that of another, whom we happen
to be more partial to. A parent, under
diftreffed circumftances, fhould be fup-
ported, even though it fhould prevent
our faving a fortune for a child; nay
more, fhould they be both in diftrefs
at the fame time, the prior obligation
fhould be firft difcharged.

Under this head may be included
the treatment of animals. Over them
many children tyrannize with impu-
nity; and find amufement in tormenting,
or wantonly killing, any infect that
comes in their way, though it does
them no injury. I am perfuaded, if
they

they were told ſtories of them, and led
to take an intereſt in their welfare and
occupations, they would be tender to
them; as it is, they think man the
only thing of conſequence in the creation. I once prevented a girl's killing ants, for ſport, by adapting Mr.
Addiſon's account of them to her underſtanding. Ever after ſhe was careful not to tread on them, leſt ſhe ſhould
diſtreſs the whole community.

Stories of inſects and animals are
the firſt that ſhould rouſe the childiſh
paſſions, and exerciſe humanity; and
then they will riſe to man, and from
him to his Maker.

CARD-

CARD-PLAYING.

CARD-playing is now the conftant
amufement, I may fay employ-
ment, of young and old, in genteel life.
After all the fatigue of the toilet,
blooming girls are fet down to card-
tables, and the moft unpleafing paffions called forth.   Avarice does not
wait for grey hairs and wrinkles, but
marks a countenance where the loves
and graces ought to revel.   The hours
that fhould be fpent in improving the
mind, or in innocent mirth, are thus
thrown away ; and if the ftake is not
confiderable enough to roufe the paffions, loft in infipidity, and a habit acquired

quired which may lead to ferious mifchief. Not to talk of gaming, many
people play for more than they can
well afford to lofe, and this fours their
temper. Cards are the univerfal refuge
to which the idle and the ignorant refort, to pafs life away, and to keep their
inactive fouls awake, by the tumult of
hope and fear.

  " Unknown to them, when fenfual plea_
   " fures cloy,
  " To fill the languid paufe with finer joy;
  " Unknown thofe powers that raife the foul
   " to flame,
  " Catch every nerve, and vibrate through
   " the frame."

And, of courfe, this is their favourite
amufement. Silent, ftupid attention
    L   appears

appears neceffary; and too frequently little arts are practifed which debafe the character, and at beft give it a trifling turn. Certainly nothing can be more abfurd than permitting girls to acquire a fondnefs for cards. In youth the imagination is lively, and novelty gives charms to every fcene; pleafure almoft obtrudes itfelf, and the pliable mind and warm affections are eafily wrought on. They want not thofe refources, which even refpectable and fenfible perfons fometimes find neceffary, when they fee life, as it is unfatisfactory, and cannot anticipate pleafures, which they know will fade when nearly viewed. Youth

I

is

is the season of activity, and should not be lost in listlessness. Knowledge ought to be acquired, a laudable ambition encouraged; and even the errors of passion may produce useful experience, expand the faculties, and teach them to know their own hearts. The most shining abilities, and the most amiable dispositions of the mind, require culture, and a proper situation, not only to ripen and improve them, but to guard them against the perversions of vice, and the contagious influence of bad examples.

L 2   THE

THE THEATRE.

THE amusements which this place afford are generally supposed the most rational, and are really so to a cultivated mind; yet one that is not quite formed may learn affectation at the theatre. Many of our admired tragedies are too full of declamation, and a false display of the passions. A heroine is often made to grieve ten or twenty years, and yet the unabated sorrow has not given her cheeks a pallid hue; she still inspires the most violent passion in every beholder, and her own yields not to time. The prominent features of a passion are easily

4   copied,

copied, while the more delicate touches are overlooked. That ſtart of Cordelia's, when her father ſays, " I think that Lady is my daughter," has affected me beyond meaſure, when I could unmoved hear Caliſta deſcribe the cave in which ſhe would live " Until her tears had waſhed her guilt away."

The principal characters are too frequently made to riſe above human nature, or ſink below it; and this occaſions many falſe concluſions. The chief uſe of dramatic performances ſhould be to teach us to diſcriminate characters; but if we reſt in ſeparat-

L 3   ing

ing the good from the bad, we are very superficial obſervers.   May I venture a conjecture?— I cannot help thinking, that every human creature has ſome ſpark of goodneſs, which their long-ſuffering and benevolent Father gives them an opportunity of improving, though they may perverſely ſmother it before they ceaſe to breathe.

Death is treated in too ſlight a manner; and ſought, when diſappointments occur, with a degree of impatience, which proves that the main end of life has not been conſidered. That fearful puniſhment of ſin, and convulſion of nature, is too often expoſed

poſed to public view. Until very lately I never had the courage even to look at a perſon dying on the ſtage. The hour of death is not the time for the diſplay of paſſions; nor do I think it natural it ſhould: the mind is then dreadfully diſturbed, and the trifling ſorrows of this world not thought of. The deaths on the ſtage, in ſpite of the boaſted ſenſibility of the age, ſeem to have much the ſame effect on a polite audience, as the execution of malefactors has on the mob that follow them to Tyburn.

The worſt ſpecies of immorality is inculcated, and life (which is to determine the fate of eternity) thrown away when

L 4 a king-

a kingdom or miſtreſs is loſt. Patience and ſubmiſſion to the will of
Heaven, and thoſe virtues which render us uſeful to ſociety, are not brought
forward to view ; nor can they occa-
ſion thoſe ſurpriſing turns of fortune
which moſt delight vulgar minds.
The almoſt imperceptible progreſs of
the paſſions, which Shakeſpeare has ſo
finely delineated, are not ſufficiently
obſerved, though the ſtart of the actor
is applauded. Few tragedies, I think,
will pleaſe a perſon of diſcernment,
and their ſenſibility is ſure to be hurt.

Young perſons, who are happily
ſituated, do well to enter into ficti-
tious

tious diſtreſs ; and if they have any judicious perſon to direct their judgment, it may be improved while their hearts are melted. Yet I would not have them confine their compaſſion to the diſtreſſes occaſioned by love ; and perhaps their feelings might more profitably be rouſed, if they were to ſee ſometimes the complicated miſery of ſickneſs and poverty, and weep for the beggar inſtead of the king.

Comedy is not now ſo cenſurable as it was ſome years ago ; and a chaſte ear is not often ſhocked with indecencies. When follies are pointed out, and vanity ridiculed, it may be

very

very improving; and perhaps the
ſtage is the only place where ridicule
is uſeful.

What I have ſaid is certainly only
applicable to thoſe who go to ſee the
play, and not to ſhew themſelves and
waſte time. The moſt inſignificant
amuſement will afford inſtruction to
thinking minds, and the moſt rational
will be loſt on a vacant one.

Remarks on the actors are frequently very tireſome. It is a fa-
ſhionable topic, and a thread-bare
one; it requires great abilities, and
a knowledge of nature, to be a com-
petent

petent judge; and thofe who do not enter into the fpirit of the author, are not qualified to converfe with confidence on the fubject.

PUBLIC

PUBLIC PLACES.

UNDER this head I rank all thofe
places, which are open to an indifcriminate refort of company. There
feems at prefent fuch a rage for pleafure, that when adverfity does not call
home the thoughts, the whole day is
moftly fpent in preparations and plans,
or in actual diffipation. Solitude appears infupportable, and domeftic
comfort ftupid. And though the a-
mufements may not always be relifh-
ed, the mind is fo enervated it cannot
exert itfelf to find out any other fub-
ftitute. An immoderate fondnefs for
drefs is acquired, and many fafhion-
able

able females spend half the night in going from one place to another to display their finery, repeat commonplace compliments, and raise envy in their acquaintance whom they endeavour to outshine. Women, who are engaged in those scenes, must spend more time in dress than they ought to do, and it will occupy their thoughts when they should be better employed.

In the fine Lady how few traits do we observe of those affections which dignify human nature! If she has any maternal tenderness, it is of a childish kind. We cannot be too careful not to verge on this character; though she

she lives many years she is still a child in understanding, and of so little use to society, that her death would scarcely be observed.

Dissipation leads to poverty, which cannot be patiently borne by those who have lived on the vain applause of others, on account of outward advantages; these were the things they imagined of most consequence, and of course they are tormented with false shame, when by a reverse of fortune they are deprived of them.

A young innocent girl, when she first enters into gay scenes, finds her

spirits

spirits so raised by them, that she would often be lost in delight, if she was not checked by observing the behaviour of a class of females who attend those places. What a painful train of reflections do then arise in the mind, and convictions of the vice and folly of the world are prematurely forced on it. It is no longer a paradise, for innocence is not there; the taint of vice poisons every enjoyment, and affectation, though despised, is very contagious. If these reflections do not occur, languor follows the extraordinary exertions, and weak minds fall a prey to imaginary distress, to banish which they are obliged to take as a remedy what produced the disease.

We

We talk of amusements unbending the mind; so they ought; yet even in the hours of relaxation we are acquiring habits. A mind accustomed to observe can never be quite idle, and will catch improvement on all occasions. Our pursuits and pleasures should have the same tendency, and every thing concur to prepare us for a state of purity and happiness. There vice and folly will not poison our pleasures; our faculties will expand, and not mistake their objects; and we shall no longer " see as through a " glass darkly, but know, even as we " are known."

F I N I S.